Police Officer

Diana Herweck

Consultants

Timothy Rasinski, Ph.D.
Kent State University

Lori Oczkus
Literacy Consultant

Joe Garcia
Police Officer, Seal Beach Police
Department

Michael Hutchinson
Detective, Long Beach Police
Department

Based on writing from
TIME For Kids. TIME For Kids and the *TIME For Kids* logo are registered trademarks of TIME Inc. Used under license.

Publishing Credits

Dona Herweck Rice, *Editor-in-Chief*
Lee Aucoin, *Creative Director*
Jamey Acosta, *Senior Editor*
Lexa Hoang, *Designer*
Stephanie Reid, *Photo Editor*
Rane Anderson, *Contributing Author*
Rachelle Cracchiolo, *M.S.Ed., Publisher*

Image Credits: pp.8, 32 –33, 48–49 Alamy;
p.22 Associated Press; pp.22–23 Corbis; pp.6–7,
12–14, 16–17, 30 Getty Images; pp.24, 26, 35 (top
left, top right) iStockphoto; p.35 (bottom
left) EyePress/Newscom; pp.18–19 imagebroker/
Jochen Tack/Newscom; pp.18, 24 REUTERS/
Newscom; pp.27, 49 UPI/Newscom; ; p.35
(bottom right) WENN.com/Newscom; pp.8–9,
11 (left middle) ZUMA Press/Newscom; pp.20,
26–27, 36–37 (illustrations) Timothy J. Bradley;
p.15 (bottom) Rio Hondo Police Academy;
p.11 (bottom) Gerald L. Nino, CBP, U.S. Dept.
of Homeland Security; All other images from
Shutterstock.

Teacher Created Materials

5301 Oceanus Drive
Huntington Beach, CA 92649-1030
http://www.tcmpub.com
ISBN 978-1-4333-4905-8
© 2013 Teacher Created Materials, Inc.

TABLE OF CONTENTS

PROTECT AND SERVE

"He's got a gun!" A call goes out to 911. The witness describes the **culprit** who fled. The **dispatchers** radio the police officers on duty. The officers turn on their sirens and rush to the scene. Half a dozen police cars pull up from all directions and screech to a halt. Help has arrived.

Police officers are trained to deal with criminals. And that's only one part of their job. Police officers protect and serve the community. They must be ready to respond to anything. They put their lives on the line to protect others. It's a dangerous job. But someone has to do it.

DO NOT CROSS POLICE LINE DO NOT CROS

British police
controlling crowds

THINK LINK

- In what ways does a police officer protect and serve the community?

- What kind of training does it take to be a police officer?

- What motivates someone to become a police officer?

DO N

THE FIRST POLICE

Today, a police force of some kind exists in nearly every country. The profession has existed for thousands of years. In ancient China, **prefects** reported crimes to a judge. In ancient Greece, slaves guarded important meetings and dealt with criminals. In Spain, people banded together to protect themselves from criminals. These peacekeepers were called the *Hermandad*, which means "brotherhood." In the 1660s, law enforcement became paid work instead of just a social duty. In 1666, France created a unified police force led by the government. Many countries followed France's example.

Arresting Origins

The word *police* comes from the ancient Greek word *polissoos*, which means "a person guarding a city."

French police officer from the 1600s

Historians note 1730 as the year the word *police* was first used. It was in Scotland, and the word meant "people who enforced the law."

LEARNING THE ROPES

Many people want to become police officers. But not all of them can handle the training. Others will fail the final test. In most places, people need to be over 21 years old to take the **entrance exam** for the **academy**. The test isn't easy. Depending on the size of the force, more than 3,000 applicants might take the test at one time. When someone passes the test, a **background check** is run. A history with gangs or even a simple traffic ticket can disqualify someone. Of the thousands who might take the test, very few will be invited to the academy.

Starting Early

Some police departments take on young **cadets**. Cadets can perform office work and take classes before they become old enough to apply for a regular police job.

The Good Citizen Award

Do you want to become a police officer? You need to stay out of trouble, follow the law, and be a good citizen, too. Police officers need to be good citizens. They need to have a clean record when applying for the police academy. The choices you make today can affect your future as an adult.

Outstanding Officers

It takes a team of professionals to make up a great police department. There are many ways to protect the community. Check out some of the ways that officers keep us safe.

The motor patrol uses a car as the main source of transportation while patrolling.

Officers on the bike patrol can fit through tight spaces where a motor patrol cannot.

Canine officers work with dogs to locate explosives, drugs, or missing people.

The Special Weapons and Tactics (SWAT) team is called in for high-risk operations.

Officers on boat patrol watch for criminals on water instead of land.

School resource officers serve as law enforcement on school campuses.

A detective carries out investigations to solve crimes.

Field officers patrol the community to keep the peace and capture criminals.

THE FIRST STEP

Being accepted into the police academy is tough. Surviving it is even tougher. Students have a lot to learn. And they must endure intense physical pain. **Recruits** must answer, "Yes, Sir!" and "No, Sir!" Every new recruit is put under a lot of stress. It's a test. Officers need to be prepared to handle the real-life stresses of the job. They will need to work long hours. There will be difficult cases. And they may need to take the lead in a violent situation. **Candidates** who can't handle the stress of the academy may need to rethink their careers.

Heads Up!

Recruits prepare for the academy ahead of time by:
- being in great physical health
- understanding how to be part of a team
- learning how to stay organized
- managing personal stress

POLICE LINE DO NOT CROSS POLICE LINE DO NOT CRO

Recruits practice restraining and arresting each other.

Some academies teach foreign languages, including Spanish and Vietnamese. It is important for officers to be able to communicate with people in the areas they serve. If you speak other languages, it may give you an edge in the academy!

AT THE ACADEMY

Life at the academy is like **boot camp**. The academy tests each candidate's strength, dedication, and courage. Each new recruit is pushed to the limit. The schedule is strict, and recruits must stay on track to keep up with their classmates.

Falling In Line

Here is what a typical day looks like for new recruits.

5:00 A.M.	Wake up.
5:30 A.M.	Eat breakfast.
6:00 A.M.	Arrive at the academy.
6:30 A.M.	Get into uniform. Prepare for **inspection**. Line up in formation.
7:00 A.M.	Inspection
7:30 A.M.	Academics
12:00 P.M.	Eat lunch with other recruits.
1:00 P.M.	Physical fitness
3:00 P.M.	Arrest techniques
4:30 P.M.	Change clothes and go home.
5:00 P.M.	Relax. Visit with family.
5:30 P.M.	Eat dinner.
6:00 P.M.	Study.
10:30 P.M.	Go to bed.

Academy students must pass a variety of tests before they can graduate.

INSIDE THE ACADEMY

Training can last six months. Some recruits don't even make it through the first day. The academy trains 40 hours a week. Recruits study **penal codes** and laws. They review the policies of their **jurisdiction**. They learn how to handle guns, write reports, and solve crimes. Recruits learn how to perform searches and make arrests. They need to be able to follow the laws. They also train physically. Recruits lift weights and run every day. There are tests every day. If recruits fail too many tests, they must leave the academy. Students must maintain at least a *B* average.

Police on the Radio

You can listen to real-life cops as they patrol the city, fighting crime. With your parent's permission, look for a website that offers streaming audio from police radios. Search online for "police live audio" or "police live radio." Some websites let you choose the state and city you listen to.

Police on TV

Many popular TV shows have featured police officers. *Law and Order* was the longest running show about law enforcement in America. New episodes were produced from 1990 to 2010. Like many crime dramas, it often showed cases being solved in 60 minutes. Real-life crimes can take weeks, months, or even years to solve.

FIREARMS

Learning to handle a weapon properly is important. If recruits aren't successful, they can't continue in the academy. Recruits must learn how to safely hold and load a gun. They learn to fire and clean it. They also learn when to use it. Officers can't be afraid to use their guns when they need protection. But they try to stay safe without using guns whenever possible. The consequences of misusing a gun can be deadly.

Recruits practice shooting targets. They start with simple targets such as posters and **mannequins**. Then, they practice on moving targets. Police officers must be ready to respond to a wide variety of situations. Recruits practice shooting in daylight and in the dark. They learn how to stop someone from taking their weapons from them. They also learn how to use their weapons to **apprehend** suspects. Officers must be able to use their weapons to protect themselves and others.

18

At the Shooting Range

Police use shooting ranges to practice working with **firearms**. Some shooting ranges look like villages or towns. Recruits and officers can practice aiming at still or moving targets. They can also see what it might be like to shoot at a gas station, grocery store, or other location.

weapons training in Germany

The Last Resort

Police use different types of weapons, including **tasers**, **pepper spray**, and **batons**. Although trained to use each of these, they only do so as a last resort.

taser

pepper spray

baton

19

Clearing the Building

It's 3 A.M. The police arrive at an abandoned office building to investigate reports of suspicious noises and lights. They approach the building carefully. Someone could be inside with a weapon.

It is important for police officers to move slowly in dangerous areas. If they are quiet and careful, they can surprise a criminal.

Police start an arm's length away from each corner, keeping their guns hidden. They scan the area from floor to ceiling with every step.

Officers quietly touch door handles to see if they are locked. Then, they push them open wide to get a clear view of the room.

Officers lead with their guns.

Officers' eyes follow the line of their gun barrels. Looking at situations this way helps police react faster in an emergency.

Police follow the edge of a hallway. They avoid open paths. They track which rooms have been cleared and which rooms may still be dangerous.

POLICE

LEARNING THE LAW

Police officers need to know the laws of their city, state, and country. Otherwise, how would they know when someone is breaking the law? In the United States, police must read all suspects their Miranda rights. This step ensures suspects understand their rights before questioning. If they don't, the information gathered by the officers can't be used in court.

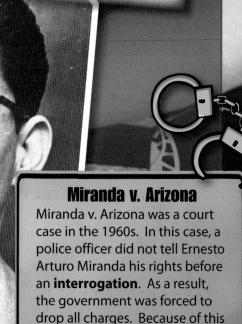

Ernesto Arturo Miranda

Miranda v. Arizona

Miranda v. Arizona was a court case in the 1960s. In this case, a police officer did not tell Ernesto Arturo Miranda his rights before an **interrogation**. As a result, the government was forced to drop all charges. Because of this case, the United States Supreme Court ruled that police must read suspects their rights.

Know Your Rights

The exact wording changes from place to place, but the Miranda rights read something like this:

*You have the right to remain silent. Anything you say or do can and will be held against you in a court of law. You have the right to speak to an **attorney**. If you cannot afford an attorney, one will be provided for you. Do you understand these rights as they have been read to you?*

JOINING THE FORCE

Only the best academy recruits graduate and become police officers. Even then, the training isn't over. **Rookie** cops are on **probation** for a year. If they do anything wrong, they could be forced to leave. During their first year, rookies are never alone. A training officer stays with them at all times. The training officer is someone with many years of experience. He or she watches as the rookie takes the lead. The training officer steps in to help when needed.

Rookies practice responding to calls and asking questions. They also make arrests and write tickets. At the end of their **shifts**, they complete paperwork and write reports. The training officers grade the rookies on their performance.

An officer writes a report.

Even after the academy, rookies must train to stay in top physical shape.

Rookie Heroes

They may be beginners, but that doesn't mean they aren't ready for the job. One rookie saved a man from a burning car. Another rookie saved a choking baby on his third day on the job. These rookies weren't seen as rookies by the community. They were seen as heroes!

The Chain of Command

There is a lot of room for growth in a police department. Over time, officers can move up in the chain of command. Whatever job they have, they will use their **field experience** and knowledge of the law as they are promoted from one job to the next.

A sergeant is in charge of training new officers. He or she makes sure policies are being followed. If a police officer breaks a rule, the sergeant determines the appropriate consequences.

A lieutenant supervises sergeants and other lower officers and manages his or her own division within the department.

A police captain reports to the chief of police and supervises equipment, people, and investigations.

The chief of police oversees the entire police department. He or she is responsible for directing all activities within the department. The chief works directly with the city manager.

The deputy chief is second in command. He or she assumes command when the chief of police is absent.

A commander plans and supervises activities for a specific division within the department.

COMMANDER

DEPUTY CHIEF

CHIEF OF POLICE

A police chief speaks with reporters.

27

SHIFT WORK

Crimes don't just happen during the day. They happen at all hours. Some crimes tend to occur around the same times. But other crimes happen throughout the day. That is why no two days are ever the same for an officer. Whether it's 5 A.M. or 3 P.M., there are always officers on duty. Depending on an officer's schedule, he or she might work an early shift, mid-day shift, or night shift. Some departments work eight-hour days. Others work 10 or 12 hours each day. A typical shift may be from 7:00 A.M. to 5:00 P.M. Those on the night shift may work 10:00 P.M. to 8:00 A.M.

Like Clockwork

Number of Crimes Reported

Even crime sleeps. Crime is least likely to occur between 3 and 6 A.M.

12 A.M.   3 A.M.   6 A.M.   9 A.M.

Graveyard Shift

In many jobs, the night shift from midnight to 8 A.M. is called the *graveyard shift*. Our bodies usually crave sleep at night, so it's a difficult time to work.

shootings and assaults

burglaries and theft

vandalism

| 12 P.M. | 3 P.M. | 6 P.M. | 9 P.M. |

POLICE LINE DO NOT CROSS

29

GEARING UP

Officers arrive at work in their own clothes. They change into their uniforms in the locker room. They must make sure their uniforms are in order. Then, they check all their equipment. If anything is wrong, they must fix it before heading out into the field. Besides a gun, officers carry handcuffs, a baton, a tape recorder, keys, extra bullets, and a flashlight. Each of these tools could save someone's life or bring someone to **justice**.

Officers prepare for duty with bulletproof vests.

Head-to-Toe Hero

Every officer carries a badge.

A bulletproof vest is worn under the shirt.

Most uniforms are made of wool. It keeps officers warm in the winter, but can be very hot in the summer.

Note cards and pens are stored in the pocket.

A radio lets an officer talk with others in the field.

The gun belt is heavy with tools and weapons.

The officer carries a knife and a back-up gun.

Heavy black boots with steel toes protect the feet.

POLICE

MORNING MEET UP

Once they are dressed, and their uniforms and gear are in order, the officers head to a **squad** meeting. The lead officer reviews what happened during the last shift. The officers learn of recent crimes and current cases. Updates are given on **search warrants** that need to be served. Uniforms and equipment may be inspected, too. The officers never know when this will take place. They must be ready every shift.

A squad trades notes.

Just as in the United States, British police officers meet at the beginning of each shift to discuss the latest events.

Patrol Prep

Before each shift, many police officers mentally prepare for what might happen in the field. To do so, they study the latest crime maps and recent crime reports. They create a plan and decide which clues to follow.

More than 900,000 officers serve in the United States. That's 1 officer for every 345 citizens.

FILL IT UP

When the meeting ends, officers head to their vehicles and prepare for the day. Some larger departments have special units that care for the patrol cars. But most officers handle their own cars. They check that the patrol car is clean and has a full tank of gas. The officers make sure they have their weapons loaded and ready. They also put their **ballistic** helmets and gas masks in place. Then, they log onto the computer inside the car.

Officers often use motorcycles instead of cars. They can be easier to steer into tight spaces, but they can't carry as much gear.

Officers on the Move

Police use cars, motorcycles, bicycles, and even horses to get around. However, these unusual rides prove that officers around the world can use just about anything to fight crime!

Camels are preferred for police work in the desert.

Snowmobiles help officers respond to emergencies on the snow or ice.

French and Chinese police may patrol on rollerblades in the cities.

Helicopters let police officers search for suspects from above.

A Mobile Office

Patrolling officers spend a lot of time in their cars. In fact, most officers spend more time in their cars than they do at their desks back at the department. Not just any car will do the job. Police cars are designed to keep officers safe and in control.

The computer checks to see if a nearby car may have been stolen. It can also tell officers if someone has a criminal record.

Bullet-proof glass and steel separate the front and back seats.

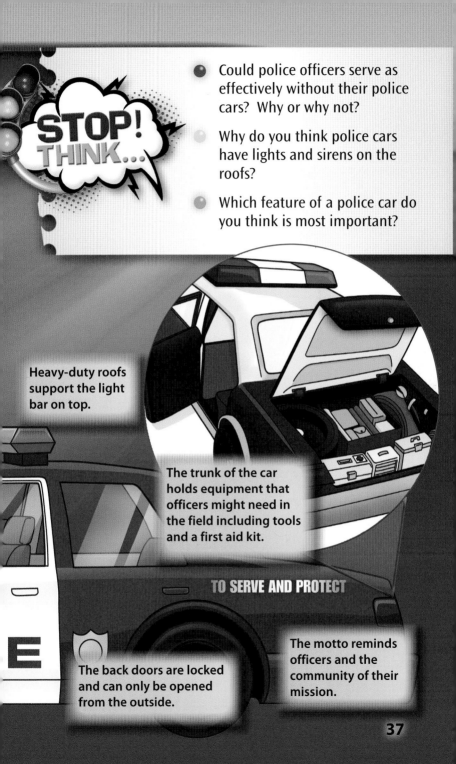

STOP! THINK...

- Could police officers serve as effectively without their police cars? Why or why not?

- Why do you think police cars have lights and sirens on the roofs?

- Which feature of a police car do you think is most important?

Heavy-duty roofs support the light bar on top.

The trunk of the car holds equipment that officers might need in the field including tools and a first aid kit.

TO SERVE AND PROTECT

E

The back doors are locked and can only be opened from the outside.

The motto reminds officers and the community of their mission.

37

DOG DETECTIVES

A police car with a picture of a dog on the door means there is a canine officer and a dog inside. Canine is another term for dog. These police units are known as *K-9* (a quick way to write canine) *units*.

Many types of dogs are used by police. The most popular kind is the German Shepherd. Dogs help with search and rescue, finding explosives, and looking for clues. Their motto could be "You can run, but you can't hide." K-9s are loved and respected by the police force. Dogs killed in the line of duty are honored by their fellow officers.

A dog sniffs luggage looking for illegal drugs and explosives.

Dogs can be trained to recognize the smell of dead bodies or to chase a criminal.

Search and rescue dogs are usually bloodhounds. These K-9 helpers are trained to find missing people, suspects, or objects. They can sniff an article of clothing that belongs to a missing person and follow the scent.

ON THE BEAT

Once the officers check their uniforms, weapons, and cars, they can head out on their **beat**. They drive around their assigned areas. It's a police officer's job to look for illegal activities. They might see someone fighting, a car accident, or even a store robbery. If they don't see anything, they might just talk with people in the neighborhood. They want to know what is happening nearby. Building good relationships encourages people to come to the police when help is needed.

Help Wanted

Since 1968, people have called *911* when they have an emergency in the United States. This telephone number works whether they need a police, fire, or ambulance response. The number is not the same in all places around the world, though.

Emergency Contacts	
Egypt	122
Hong Kong	999
Norway	112
Australia	000
Mexico	066
Barbados	211
Peru	105

HELP!

If you are traveling to a new country, it's a good idea to look up the emergency telephone number ahead of time.

AT THE SCENE

Police officers are called when a crime happens in their beat. It's their job to get to the scene quickly and start investigating. They talk with the victims. They find witnesses. If the suspect is present, the officers begin asking questions. They also collect evidence. And if they need extra help, they call a crime scene investigator (CSI). When the detectives arrive on the scene, the officers update them on what they have learned so far.

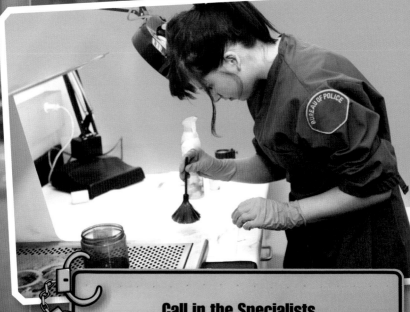

Call in the Specialists

CSIs are called when special assistance is needed. They help collect evidence, lift prints, take pictures, and more. Depending on the area, they may work in the city's crime lab, too.

On the Beat

Many cities have beat maps online that tell you what patrol area you live in and which officers are assigned to your neighborhood.

World Crime Rates

The United States has one of the highest crime rates in the world. Americans make up less than five percent of the world's population. But 18 percent of total crimes reported in the world happen in the United States. Check out the number of crimes reported each year.

Canada
2,500,000

United States
12,000,000

Brazil
5,600,000

Some countries may be home to high crime rates, but many crimes may not be reported. This map only compares the rate of crimes that are reported.

Russia
2,900,000

United Kingdom
6,500,000

Japan
2,800,000

Italy
2,200,000

India
1,800,000

South Africa
2,700,000

PICKING UP THE PIECES

Officers spend many hours patrolling in their cars. When a crime happens, they race to the scene. But their work doesn't stop there. After hours on the street, they write detailed case reports. Later, a detective follows up and investigates further if needed. If a suspect has been arrested, police officers have three days to present their case to the **District Attorney**. This determines if charges will be filed. There is a lot of work to do in only 72 hours. If the work isn't done correctly, the suspect can be released. The smallest detail might be what is needed to put a criminal behind bars.

Police Reports

Arrest reports and crime reports are the main reports officers write. Arrest reports give details on arrests made by police officers. Crime or incident reports provide details about how police handled an incident. They may detail how an officer responded to a call for assistance, an accident occurred, or crimes were committed.

Inside an Incident Report

Reporting Officer: Jonathan Smith	Date and Time: 06/15/13 at 19:32		
Incident Type:	Place of Occu... 1329 Oak Park		
	Sex: F	Race: Asian	27
Suspect(s) or Description(s): #1: 6'2", stocky build, blond spiky hair, wearing blue cap, gray T-shirt, and jeans #2: 5'9", thin, bla... hair, wearing black sweatshirt and jean...	Sex: M M	Race: White Asian	Age: 20s 20s
Vehicle Description: None	Weapon(s) Used: Knife		

Officers don't use slang terms in reports.

The date, time, and other details are recorded.

Reports include descriptions of the victim and suspect.

Narrative:
The victim was walking her dog in the park when two men approached her. Suspect #1 held out a knife. He told the victim to give him her money. Suspect #2 stood behind the victim to block her escape. The victim gave Suspect #1 her purse and jewelry. A witness heard the victim's dog barking and approached. Suspects fled southbound on foot. No injuries to victim.

The narrative is written in simple, formal language.

THE CALL OF DUTY

It's never too early to start training for a career in law enforcement. You can start now. Police officers need to know and follow all the laws. You can start by following the rules in your school. Officers write reports every day. So, it's important to practice reading and writing. Often, police reports are read by lawyers and judges. They might even make their way all the way up to the Supreme Court.

The police academy is tough. So plan to go to college and earn a degree. This will help you develop study skills that will be useful in the academy.

Physical training starts with a healthy diet and exercise every day. Everyone, from bike cops to detectives, needs to be able to hit the ground running when a crime occurs. Officers train to be in top shape. You can start building your strength now.

Explorer Scouts

Boys and girls between 14 and 21 years old can join Explorer Scouts. Explorers train for police work. They learn about traffic stops, traffic accidents, first aid, **hostage negotiation**, and more. They help with special events and go on police ride-alongs. If you are interested in policing, you might consider joining when you are 14.

Explorer Scouts prepare supplies for a new mission.

DIG DEEPER!

Cop Codes

Police officers use codes to communicate quickly and secretly over radios. They must remember dozens of codes and be ready to use them at any moment. Check out the codes below to see which ones you can memorize.

10-6 Standby for more information.

10-16 A vehicle has been reported stolen.

10-10 A crime may have been committed.

10-12 A police officer is holding a suspect for questioning.

WORKING TOGETHER

Police officers share similar beliefs and experiences. They train and work long hours together. They rely on each other every day. Over time, they become close. Members of a department have a special bond with one another. They share a sense of **camaraderie**. They work together best when they are trusted friends. And after the long hours and dedication they put in, police work is more than a career. It becomes an officer's **identity**. A police officer is never really off duty.

Friends of the Force

If you like law enforcement but don't think you want to be a police officer, there are many other jobs you could try. You could be a security guard, join the military police, or become an agent with the Federal Bureau of Investigation (FBI). You could even be a private investigator.

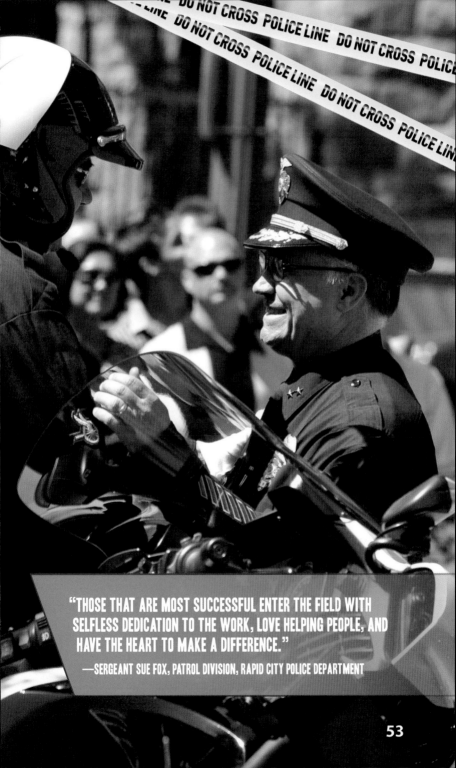

"THOSE THAT ARE MOST SUCCESSFUL ENTER THE FIELD WITH SELFLESS DEDICATION TO THE WORK, LOVE HELPING PEOPLE, AND HAVE THE HEART TO MAKE A DIFFERENCE."

—SERGEANT SUE FOX, PATROL DIVISION, RAPID CITY POLICE DEPARTMENT

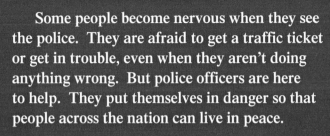

Some people become nervous when they see the police. They are afraid to get a traffic ticket or get in trouble, even when they aren't doing anything wrong. But police officers are here to help. They put themselves in danger so that people across the nation can live in peace.

For thousands of years, police work has made our cities safer. Police officers are brave **first responders**. They keep the peace, patrol in the dark of night, and look for trouble before it strikes. They put their lives on the line to protect and serve their communities. Without them, the world would be a different place.

DIG DEEPER!

Meet a Police Officer

Meet Detective Michael Hutchinson, a police officer in the Long Beach Police Department in California. He has over 10 years of experience. He sat down with writer Diana Herweck to share his thoughts on his job.

Diana: Why did you become a police officer?

Det. Hutchinson: Ever since I was five, it was the only thing I wanted to do.

Diana: What would you tell someone who is thinking about becoming a police officer?

Det. Hutchinson: Take school seriously. Do well in English because the majority of the job is writing reports.

Diana: What degree should someone get?

Det. Hutchinson: Many people think they should get a degree in criminal justice, but you'll learn to be a police officer when you get the job. Because of the way the world is going, I think a technology degree would be very helpful.

Diana: What is the best thing about being a police officer?

Det. Hutchinson: Every day is different. You never know what to expect, so the job doesn't get boring.

Diana: Are there any bad things about being a police officer?

Det. Hutchinson: It's hard when I see bad things happen to people, and I can't do anything about it. But most of the time when bad things happen, I can do something about it.

Diana: What is one of the memorable or funny cases you've worked?

Det. Hutchinson: My family will never let me forget when I was bitten by a dog. An elderly lady was being attacked and I pulled the attacker off. When I did that, her dog broke through the screen door and bit me. I had to go to the doctor, and I had a full set of bite marks on my rear end.

57

GLOSSARY

academy—an institution, or school, for training in special subjects or skills

apprehend—to take into custody; arrest by legal warrant or authority

attorney—a lawyer, an expert on legal rights and laws

background check—to investigate someone's origin, education, and experience

ballistic—having to do with firearms

batons—clubs used for defense

beat—a police officer's regular route or path

boot camp—a place where new members of the military receive intensive training

cadets—young people who begin training with a police department before they are old enough to become officers

camaraderie—good feelings between people in a group

candidates—people who are being considered for a job

canine—another word for dog

culprit—one accused of or charged with a crime

dispatchers—people who quickly send out police officers to a crime scene

District Attorney—a lawyer for the people or government within a specific area

entrance exam—an examination to determine a person's preparation for a course of studies

field experience—time spent serving the community, working with people on the beat, and learning the job

firearms—weapons from which a shot is discharged by gunpowder

first responders—people trained to be the first at the scene of an emergency

hostage negotiation—a technique used by law enforcement to communicate with people who have taken others against their will

identity—a person's sense of who he or she is based on personal beliefs and values

inspection—the act of looking at something especially carefully or critically

interrogation—a session of formal and thorough questioning

jurisdiction—an area in which someone has the power to carry out justice

justice—the fair and moral punishment and reward of people

mannequins—human figures used to model clothes and stand in for people in dangerous situations

penal codes—documents that include most or all of a jurisdiction's laws

pepper spray—a substance that causes pain and blindness when sprayed at an attacker

prefects—people appointed to positions of command

probation—the testing of a person's conduct for a specific period of time

recruits—new members of a group

rookie—beginner

search warrants—documents giving power to an officer to search a person's body or home

shifts—periods of time during which people work

squad—a group of police officers

tasers—guns that fire electric darts instead of bullets

INDEX

BIBLIOGRAPHY

Judah, Christy. *Meet the Police Dogs: The K-9 Cop.*
CreateSpace, 2009.

Meet specially trained police dogs across the country that
help officers solve cases involving robberies, fires, bombs,
illegal drugs, and more. This book will help you understand
why it is important to obey the law and appreciate our police
officers and K-9 cops.

Lane, Brian and Laura Buller. *DK Eyewitness Books:
Crime & Detection.* DK Children, 2005.

Discover how the most infamous crimes in history were
carried out and the techniques used to solve these cases.
These true stories range from piracy and international
gangsters to theft and murder.

Lewis, Barbara A. *The Kid's Guide to Service Projects:
Over 500 Service Ideas for Young People Who Want to
Make a Difference.* Free Spirit Publishing, 2009.

You're not a police officer yet, but it's never too soon to
help out! Try one of the service project ideas in this book
to fight crime, promote safety, or make a difference in your
neighborhood.

Scott, Carey. *Crime Scene Detective.* DK Children,
2009.

Solve four crimes—robbery, arson, forgery, and murder—by
studying the clues, collecting evidence, cracking the case,
and catching the suspects. Do-it-yourself activities help you
understand the science behind forensic investigations.

Wiese, Jim. *Detective Science: 40 Crime-Solving,
Case-Breaking, Crook-Catching Activities for Kids.* John
Wiley & Sons, Incorporated, 1996.

Find out how to dust for fingerprints, analyze handwriting,
tail suspects, and complete other activities that will teach
you how to crack down on crime.

MORE TO EXPLORE

Be a Junior Detective!
http://familyfun.go.com/playtime/be-a-junior-detective-706968

Here you'll learn how to lift a footprint, match teeth marks, analyze handwriting, make your own detective kit, and more! You'll also get tips on laying traps for anyone who dares to sneak into your room when you're not around.

CSI: Web Adventures
http://forensics.rice.edu

Learn the science of police work and solve cases with these online games. You will get to be a rookie crime scene investigator that works with fellow CSI agents from the popular television show! Click on *Fun Stuff* for additional goodies.

Law Enforcement Career Exploring
http://exploring.learningforlife.org/services/career-exploring/law-enforcement

Interested in a career in law enforcement? Learn about the Learning for Life program open to students ages 14 to 20. Young explorers get hands-on career experience and gain leadership skills through ride-alongs in police vehicles, pistol shooting, and more.

Police Dogs
http://www.ducksters.com/animals/policedogs.php

Learn about different types of police dogs, from trackers to substance detectors, and dogs that help maintain order. You'll also learn which dog breeds make good police dogs and what happens to police dogs after they retire.

Police Officer
http://www.bls.gov/k12/law01.htm

This website helps you explore career information from the Bureau of Labor Statistics. Get the latest numbers on how much police officers are paid, how many jobs are out there, and the future of employment for police officers and detectives.

ABOUT THE AUTHOR

Diana Herweck has always been interested in the things people do, including their jobs. She counts many police officers as friends. She also loves working with children and spending time with her family. She enjoys playing with her kids, reading, music, movies, and crafts of all sorts, especially scrapbooking. Diana lives in Southern California with her husband, two wonderful children, and three dogs.